The Testimony of the Patristic Age
Concerning Mary's Death

Woodstock Papers

Occasional Essays for Theology

PREPARED BY

Professors of the Faculty of Theology
Woodstock College, Woodstock, Maryland

EDITED BY

JOHN COURTNEY MURRAY, S.J.
WALTER J. BURGHARDT, S.J.

No. 2

THE NEWMAN PRESS

WESTMINSTER, MARYLAND

1957

The Testimony

of the

Patristic Age Concerning

Mary's Death

by Walter J. Burghardt, S.J.

Professor of Patrology and Patristic Theology

Woodstock College

THE NEWMAN PRESS

WESTMINSTER, MARYLAND

1957

⋆ Contents ⋆

I

⋆ Introduction ⋆

One of the more exciting by-products of the definition of our Lady's Assumption in 1950 has been a revival of interest in the question: did our Lady die? Even as an exercise in historical analysis, the problem has more than a purely antiquarian value. But its more authentic significance lies in its theological resonance: it has implications for the Christian understanding of original sin and its effects, for the precise modalities of Mary's coredemptive function, for a rounded appreciation of her Assumption. It even has eschatological import; for a solution of the problem would cast light on the role of death in the Christian economy.

An adequate approach to the problem, an informed solution, demands the investigation of all the pertinent data, the exploitation of the resources of positive and speculative theology. Because of its closeness to the event, the testimony of the patristic age, of the first seven or eight centuries, merits an early claim on our attention. More importantly, given the context of Catholic theology and its sources, an investigation of ancient Christian tradition is indispensable.

To evaluate adequately the evidence of the patristic age on the migration of Mary from this life, it is advisable to consider in successive stages (1) the Fathers and ecclesiastical writers before Ephesus, (2) the apocryphal accounts called *Transitus Mariae,* (3) the early Feast of the Dormition in East and West, (4) the Greek homiletic literature of the seventh and eighth centuries, (5) the Western witnesses from Ephesus to Bede, and (6) the tradition of the Virgin's tomb in Jerusalem and in Ephesus.[1]

The Testimony of the Patristic Age
Concerning Mary's Death

⋆ 1 ⋆

Fathers and Ecclesiastical Writers
Before Ephesus

The patristic evidence before the Council of Ephesus (431) is, on the whole, disappointing and inconclusive. The names that confront us are significant: in the East, Origen and Ephraem, Gregory of Nyssa and Severian of Gabala, Epiphanius of Salamis and Timothy of Jerusalem; in the West, Hippolytus, Ambrose, Jerome, Paulinus, and Augustine. Geographically they cover a striking cross section of the Christian world. But the evidence they provide is not proportionately important. Pertinent passages are relatively rare; the references to our problem are usually oblique; the mind of the author is frequently debatable; and three pieces of evidence are complicated by questions of genuinity.

Before Nicaea the only overt reference to the close of our Lady's earthly life is a phrase attributed to Origen († 253): "With respect to the brethren of Jesus (cf. Jn 2:12), there are many who ask how He had them, seeing that Mary remained a virgin until her death."[2] The passage, whose authenticity is suspect, is more significant as testimony to Mary's permanent virginity than as evidence for her death. True, her death is mentioned obliquely, as though it were self-evident, with no consciousness of con-

[3]

troversy. But this manner of speaking need not reflect a tradition; it may stem, as Jugie suspects, from lack of reflection on the dignity of God's Mother. In a word, we may conclude no more than that the author took our Lady's death for granted.[3]

A strophe from the Marian hymns of Ephraem († 373) sings with Syrian frankness: "A virgin gave Him birth and kept her genitalia intact. She bent low to give Him birth and is a virgin; she rose up to give Him milk and is a virgin. She died and her genitalia were not unlocked."[4] Ephraem's concern, like Origen's, is Mary's perpetual virginity. To that end, again like Origen, he affirms Mary's death in passing, as a self-evident phenomenon, in no need of justification. The affirmation is subordinate, perhaps heedless, certainly unique in Ephraem; but the affirmation is there.[5]

The mind of Gregory of Nyssa is more elusive. Writing on virginity about 370, he compares the Virgin with other virgins, to illustrate the victory of virginity over death. The ordinary virgin destroys death's power by refusing to give it fresh victims; the Virgin Mary triumphed over death by giving birth virginally to Christ. "With reference to Mary, God's Mother, the death which held sway from Adam to her—for it was near her too—first stumbled on the fruit of her virginity as on some rock, and was shattered on her. . . ."[6] Despite surface impressions, two extreme conclusions must be avoided. On the one hand, Gregory does not affirm Mary's death: death came "near" Mary, reached her, not by possessing her but in attacking the fruit of her womb. On the other hand, Gregory does not deny Mary's death: death "was shattered on her" not by her personal, isolated triumph over it but in the sense that the fruit of her womb crushed death by escaping the corruption of the tomb. It may be that Gregory, like Origen and Ephraem, takes our Lady's death for granted; but, unlike Origen and Ephraem, he does not mention it.[7] In date, the last death with which the text is concerned is the death of Christ.

Seven years later the most significant testimony before Ephesus burst from Salamis, the metropolitan see of Cyprus. In a digression typical of his *Medicine Chest* against eighty heresies, Epiphanius is concerned to forestall a perilous accommodation of Jn 19:27. He is afraid that in the John-Mary relationship clerics may find a pseudo-justification for retaining in their homes the much-discussed *virgines subintroductae*. He insists that the case of Mary was guided by a wise providence, that this procedure is to be regarded as an exception to the common conduct of Christians, and that once John had taken Mary into his home she did not remain with him any longer. And he continues:

But if some think us mistaken, let them search the Scriptures. They will not find Mary's death; they will not find whether she died or did not die; they will not find whether she was buried or was not buried. More than that: John journeyed to Asia, yet nowhere do we read that he took the holy Virgin with him. Rather, Scripture is absolutely silent [on the end of Mary], because of the extraordinary nature of the prodigy, in order not to shock the minds of men.

For my own part, I do not dare to speak, but I keep my own thoughts and I practice silence. For it may be that somewhere we have found hints that it is impossible to discover the death of the holy, blessed one. On the one hand, you see, Simeon says of her, "And your own soul a sword shall pierce, that the thoughts of many hearts may be revealed" (Lk 2:35). On the other hand, when the Apocalypse of John says, "And the dragon hastened against the woman who had brought forth the male child, and there were given to her an eagle's wings, and she was carried off into the wilderness, that the dragon might not seize her" (Ap 12:13–14), it may be that this is fulfilled in her.

However, I do not assert this absolutely, and I do not say that she remained immortal; but neither do I maintain stoutly that she died. The fact is, Scripture has outstripped the human mind and left [this matter] uncertain, for the sake of that valued vessel without compare, to prevent anyone from harboring carnal thoughts in her regard. Did she die? We do not know. At all events, if she was buried, she had had no carnal intercourse. . . .[8]

Twelve chapters later Epiphanius returns succinctly to the problem of Mary's end:

. . . either the holy Virgin died and was buried; then her falling asleep was with honor, her death chaste, her crown that of virginity. Or she was killed, as it is written: "And your own soul a sword shall pierce"; then her glory is among the martyrs and her holy body amid blessings, she through whom light rose over the world. Or she remained alive, since nothing is impossible with God and He can do whatever He desires; for her end no one knows.[9]

The testimony of Epiphanius is crucial for two reasons. Before Ephesus he alone deals expressly with the problem of our Lady's passing; and he knows the Holy City and its traditions as few others of his time. The passages bristle with difficulties, especially in the matter of Epiphanius' mind on Mary's Assumption, but on our limited problem his testimony is clear enough. How did Mary end her life? Epiphanius does not know. There are three possibilities:

[6]

natural death, bloody martyrdom, deathless immortality. Of these, he insists, it is illegitimate to exclude any, illegitimate to impose any.[10] In any event, the end of Mary's life was worthy of God and in harmony with her dignity and holiness. The importance of this testimony is manifold: (a) Epiphanius is the first to pose the final destiny of Mary as a problem; (b) he has discovered its roots in the reticence of Scripture; (c) he has allowed us to glimpse the possible solutions; and (d) his evidence emphasizes the absence of a fixed historical tradition in Palestinian circles on the post-Pentecostal lot of Mary. It may well be that the three hypotheses of Epiphanius reflect three opinions held in orthodox circles.[11]

At first glance the one apodictic pre-Ephesus affirmation of Mary's exemption from death derives from a homily on Simeon by a certain Timothy, who is styled by the best manuscripts "a priest of Jerusalem" and on internal testimony was located by Jugie towards the end of the fourth century or at the beginning of the fifth.[12] From the text as reconstituted by Faller we gather that

some have supposed that the Mother of the Lord was put to death with a sword and won for herself a martyr's end. Their reason lies in the words of Simeon, "And your own soul a sword shall pierce." But such is not the case. A metal sword, you see, cleaves the body; it does not cut the soul in two. Therefore the Virgin is immortal to this day, seeing that He who had dwelt in her transported her to the regions of her assumption [OR: to the places of His ascension; OR: into the regions high above].[13]

For our purposes, Timothy's testimony is significant on two counts. In the first place, it furnishes further evidence of an

early Christian belief that our Lady died a violent death—
a conviction based on a controverted exegesis of Lk 2:35.
Second, and more troublesome, is the assertion that "the
Virgin is immortal to this day" (*hē parthenos achri tēs
deuro athanatos*). Scholars find the phrase susceptible of
several interpretations. (1) In Jugie's understanding of text
and context, Mary did not die and will not die.[14] (2) For
Capelle, Mary did not die but still can.[15] (3) In Faller's
exegesis, Mary is alive now in body and soul, and will con-
tinue to be; Timothy neither affirms nor denies that death
preceded her assumption.[16] Each exegesis is well reasoned
but none is compelling. Regrettably, the text and its problems have lost some of their pertinence and fascination ever
since Capelle argued so convincingly that "Timothy of
Jerusalem" is an unknown author of the Byzantine world,
possibly Egypt, who wrote between the sixth century and
the eighth.[17]

While developing the classical Eve-Mary parallelism,
Severian, Bishop of Gabala in Syria († after 408), pictures
Eve hearing herself constantly called a sorry, pitiful thing,
while Mary each day hears herself called blessed. It is not
only now that she is aware of such felicitation, "seeing that
she is in the place of brightness, in the land of the living.
. . . In point of fact, while she was yet living in the flesh
she was called blessed; for she heard felicitation while still
in flesh."[18] For us, the crux is the adverbial clause, "while
she was yet living in the flesh." In its obvious implications it
suggests a moment when Mary ceased living in the flesh,
when spirit was severed from flesh, when Mary died. It
seems less likely that the expression is sheerly a synonym for
"while she was yet on earth," that the contrast is simply
between life in this world and life in the next, with no over-
tones of death.

[8]

So much for the East; the contribution of the West is more scanty still. A fragment from Hippolytus (✝ *ca.* 236) asserts that "the Lord was sinless, because in His humanity He was fashioned out of incorruptible wood (*ek tōn asēptōn xylōn*), that is to say, out of the Virgin and the Holy Spirit. . . ."[19] Our Lady is called incorruptible; and the quality in question is doubtless physical. But to suggest that the writer has in mind a deathless immortality or a posthumous incorruption would be ill-advised. The text simply affirms that the Word enfleshed was sinless because He was virginally conceived.[20]

Ambrose (✝ 397), whose Mariology is as dear to the West as Ephraem's is to the East, is surprisingly taciturn on Mary's passing. Discussing Simeon's sword of sorrow, he declares that "neither Scripture nor history tells us that Mary quit this life by suffering a violent death of the body." It is Mary's soul that is pierced; but a soul is not pierced by a material sword. Simeon's sword is Mary's understanding of the mystery of her Son, an intelligence achieved through revelation.[21] But Ambrose does not tell us just how Mary did leave this life. It may be that we can read his mind on that matter in a rather remarkable text:

The Son hung on the cross; the mother offered herself to the persecutors. If this were all, a desire to be destroyed before her Son, we should have to praise the motherly love that moved her, her unwillingness to survive her Son. But if her desire was to die at the same time as her Son, she longed passionately to rise with Him; for she was not ignorant of the mystery, that her Child would rise again. Knowing, too, that the death of her Son was being expended for the common good, she stood ready to add something by her death, if it could be done, to the gift that was given for the benefit of all. But the passion of Christ had no need of assistance. . . .[22]

[9]

Ambrose, one might reason, takes for granted the sheer fact that Mary died; what mystifies him is the motivation of Mary in offering herself to death. The reasoning is not without merit; but the passage is so thoroughly hypothetical that the apodictic is to be avoided.

Jerome († 419 or 420) is puzzling for a different reason. In his polemic against Rufinus he asks "the question to which Origen answers no: Does the resurrection take place in the same sex in which the bodies have died? Does Mary rise as Mary, John as John. . . ?"[23] A parallel anti-Origenistic passage is discoverable in Jerome's book against John of Jerusalem: "A genuine resurrection is unintelligible apart from flesh and bones, apart from blood and limbs. Where you have flesh and bones, blood and limbs, there you must have different sexes. Where the sexes are different, there John is John, Mary is Mary."[24] The pertinent assertion is this: Mary rises from the dead as Mary. The pertinent question is this: Is Jerome's "Mary'" the Mother of Jesus? A negative answer is imperative if Jerome has no specific individuals in mind but is simply employing two proper names, John and Mary, as examples, much as the Catholic casuist makes use of Titius and Bertha; and such could be the case. That he may have flesh-and-blood persons in mind is suggested (but no more) by a third, analogous text in which Jerome changes one of his proper nouns so as to say: "the Apostle is [still] the Apostle, and Mary is Mary."[25] Here again, the evidence is much too thin for a hard and fast conclusion.[26]

Paulinus, Bishop of Nola in Italy († 431), is anxious to learn Augustine's mind on the exegesis of Simeon's prophecy; he himself, like Ambrose, is aware of no document reporting Mary's death by violence.[27] In his reply,

[10]

Augustine mentions a previous letter of his own on the Lucan text; it is, regrettably, lost to us; but he does tell Paulinus that their views on the scriptural passage coincide.[28] Elsewhere, in several striking phrases, Augustine makes it clear that Mary did die. She died after her Son: "He entrusts mother to disciple . . . destined as He is to die before His mother, destined to rise before His mother's death. . . ." She died a virgin: "virgin in conceiving, virgin when bearing, virgin at death." She died, like Adam, as a victim of his sin: "Mary, sprung from Adam, died in consequence of sin; Adam died in consequence of sin; and the flesh of the Lord, sprung from Mary, died to destroy sin."[29]

On the eve of Ephesus, therefore, it is difficult to lay hold of the Church's mind from the works of the Fathers and ecclesiastical writers. The death of Mary is assumed by Origen, asserted by Ephraem and Augustine, questioned by Epiphanius, perhaps denied by Timothy, while the views of Gregory of Nyssa and Severian of Gabala, Ambrose and Jerome and Paulinus, are debatable. There is evidence, too, of a fairly widespread conviction, based on Lk 2:35, that our Lady died a violent death—a conviction that met resistance on exegetical grounds and the silence of history. It may be that, preoccupied with more fundamental facets of Christian belief, the early Church, with few exceptions, took our Lady's death for granted.[30] If so, the attitude is understandable and of itself involves no immutable theological commitment; but the attitude is there, an initial segment of the total picture we are endeavoring to recapture.

★ 2 ★

Transitus Mariae Literature

A second stage in the Christian effort to fathom our Lady's destiny confronts us in the apocryphal *Transitus Mariae*.[31] The genesis of these accounts is shrouded in history's mist. They apparently originated before the close of the fifth century, perhaps in Egypt, perhaps in Syria, in consequence of the stimulus given Marian devotion by the definition of the divine maternity at Ephesus. The period of proliferation is the sixth century. More than a score of *Transitus* accounts are extant, in Greek, Arabic, Syriac, Ethiopic, Coptic, Armenian, and Latin. Not all are prototypes; many are simply variations on more ancient models.[32]

What do the *Transitus* stories say? In point of fact, the divergences are so pronounced that the accounts cannot be reduced to a genuine unity. Significantly, however, a first common feature is that all recount the death of Mary; this is their theme, their primary concern, the event which invests them with a specious homogeneity. Around this central phenomenon several characteristic, legendary details are grouped: the miraculous arrival of all or some of the Apostles; the tidings brought to Mary of her approaching death; Mary's experience of fear; some hostile Jewish intervention on the occasion of her burial. A glance at a cross section of these narratives will concretize their central theme and their geographical spread.

In the Greek apocryphon of Ps.-John the Evangelist, *On the Dormition of the Holy Mother of God,* Christ assures Mary: "From this time forth your revered body will be transposed to paradise, but your holy soul will be in the heavens, in the treasuries of my Father, in surpassing brightness. . . ."[33] Her actual death is unmistakably told:

And stretching out His unstained hands, the Lord received her holy and spotless soul. And at the departure of her spotless soul the place was filled with a sweet odor and inexpressible light. And behold, a voice from heaven was heard, saying: "Blessed are you among women." And Peter ran, and I, John, and Paul and Thomas, and embraced her precious feet to receive sanctification; and the twelve Apostles laid her honorable and holy body upon a bed and bore it forth.[34]

An Arabic offspring of the Greek Ps.-John, part translation, part interpolation, proposes its theme unambiguously in a prologue:

With the help of the most high God and under His distinguished guidance we begin our story of the falling asleep of our Lady, the pure and holy Virgin Mary, Mother of our Lord and God, our Saviour Jesus Christ. We shall relate how she departed this perishable world, for life eternal and for happiness never-ending, on the twenty-first of the month tubah [January 29]. May her prayers protect us from all the temptations of the perverted devil. Amen.[35]

In a Syriac fragment we have the epilogue of an account which Jugie considers the most ancient *Transitus* extant. These *Obsequies of the Holy Virgin* begin after the burial of Mary; there is no doubt that she has died:

And the Lord said to Michael: "Let them bring the body of Mary into the clouds." And when the body of Mary had been brought into the clouds, Our Lord said to the Apostles that they should draw near to the clouds. And when they drew near to the clouds they were singing with the voice of angels. And Our Lord told the clouds to go to the gate of paradise. And when they had entered paradise, the body of Mary went to the tree of life; and they brought her soul and made it enter her body.[36]

An Ethiopic legend, which does little more than translate a Syriac account, presents vividly the fear of Mary in the face of death. It represents our Lord giving command to Peter to see to it that all creatures of heaven and earth sing a psalm of joy and gladsomeness, and it adds: "At that moment the spirit of Mary went forth and was brought to the treasuries of the Father. Then John, stretching forth his hand, arranged Mary fittingly and closed her eyes. Peter and Paul arranged her hands and feet properly. . . ."[37]

The Coptic accounts have this added interest, that some give reasons for the death of Mary. In the Bohairic discourse of Theodosius, Jacobite Patriarch of Alexandria (✝ 567 or 568), *On the Falling Asleep of Mary,* our Lady checks the grief of the Apostles with the question: "Is it not written that all flesh must needs taste death? I also must needs return to the earth, as all the inhabitants of earth."[38] In greater detail Jesus explains to His mother:

O my beautiful mother, when Adam transgressed my commandment, I passed upon him a sentence, saying: "Adam, you are earth and you shall return unto the earth again. For I too, the Life of all men, tasted death in the flesh which I took from you, in the flesh of Adam, your forefather. But because my Godhead was united to it, for that reason I raised it from the dead. I

[15]

would prefer not to have you taste death, but to translate you up to the heavens like Enoch and Elias. But these also, even they must at last taste death. But if this happened to you, wicked men would think concerning you that you are a power which came down from heaven, and that this dispensation took place in appearance alone. . . .[39]

Mary experiences death (a) because her flesh is the flesh of condemned Adam, and (b) because a deathless translation to heaven might prove an argument for the unreality of the Incarnation.

An Armenian account of Mary's dormition has unusual interest because Gabriel promises that, in virtue of her virginal maternity and her fulness of grace, our Lady's death will necessarily differ from the death of others:

The time for your decease has come, and for your rest in the place prepared, inaccessible to men. . . . And you are departing from earth without difficulty, not like the rest of those who sleep, because your departure and theirs is dissimilar; for you gave birth in wondrous wise and did not lose your virginity. Never, you see, in times remote or recent has there appeared in the ranks of men a Virgin Mother of God, never a spiritual child-bearing. In like fashion, your departure too, and the rest that is your falling asleep, has been changed by reason of the fulness of grace that genuinely belongs to you, O Virgin most holy. For this reason sorrow and anguish have vanished from you. And it is hard to know what to say of the place, inexpressible and so delightful, which the Lord has prepared for you and in which glory follows upon glory without interruption. In utter joy, therefore, rejoice over the delights to come, O Virgin most holy, and do not be terrified by [the thought of] a cruel death; for I am not come to fill you with fright, but to remove fear of death from you; for the Lord Himself, your only-begotten Son, will lead you, O Virgin most holy, with heaven's ranks and angel choirs to rest eternal.[40]

The most important Latin account, the *Transitus* of Ps.-Melito, is equally unambiguous:

Rising from the pavement, Mary lay down on her bed; giving thanks to God, she sent forth her spirit. Now the Apostles saw her soul of such whiteness that no tongue of mortal men can fittingly express it. . . . Then the Saviour spoke, saying: "Arise, Peter, take the body of Mary and bear it to the right-hand section of the city towards the east; there you will find a new sepulchre; place it therein and wait until I come to you." So saying, the Lord delivered the soul of holy Mary to Michael. . . .[41]

As history, the *Transitus* accounts are ambivalent. From one standpoint they are valueless: they provide no credible evidence which the historian, exercising his proper craft, may employ to determine whether our Lady died.[42] And yet, these legends may not be disregarded. They witness to an historical fact which gives rise to two problems of authentic interest to the theologian. The historical fact is a conviction among Christians that the Mother of God died. The conviction is widespread in East and West; it covers several centuries; it influenced homiletic literature, early art, and the liturgy; there is no contradictory tradition to offset it. The first problem: Do the apocrypha imply an earlier tradition to which all are captive? The remarkable unanimity of the *Transitus* stories on the single issue of our Lady's death strongly suggests such a tradition, though it does not imperiously demand it.[43] The second problem: Are we confronted with a *sensus fidelium*? I submit that such an inference would be illegitimate, first, because the extent of this conviction is not sufficiently in evidence; second, and more importantly, because the conviction is not demonstrably indicative of magisterial teaching. But though the conviction that our Lady died may not be normative for Christian belief, it does exist, and at the close of the seventh century it is, the apocrypha reveal, in peaceful possession.

★ 3 ★

Feast of the Dormition

A third source of information on the destiny of Mary as envisaged in the patristic age is the early liturgy—specifically, the Feast of Our Lady's Dormition. Unfortunately, the story of that feast has not yet been satisfactorily reconstructed. This much, however, can be said: the story begins in the East, and from the East it leads by labyrinthine ways to the West.[44]

In the East, evidence of a feast unmistakably consecrated to the dormition of Mary is not discoverable till the sixth century.[45] It apparently made its initial appearance in the second half of that century in the Syrian Jacobite Church.[46] With little delay the Coptic Monophysite Church, under the Patriarch Theodosius, transformed the more primitive, less specific Commemoration of Mary into a patent feast of her death (January 16), and created a special solemnity of her bodily resurrection and glorious Assumption (August 9).[47] The Abyssinian Church, vassal daughter of the Coptic, adopted the twofold feast in short order.[48] For the orthodox or Chalcedonian Byzantine Church, the crucial date is the twilight of the same century, *ca.* 600; the decisive document is the decree of Emperor Maurice (582–602) imposing August 15 for the celebration of the dormition of God's Mother.[49] Here the scholarly puzzle is the Emperor's purpose. Did the decree genuinely transform the fifth-century Commemoration into a Feast of the Dormition properly so called, or did it merely uniformalize dormition feasts which already existed? The present state of the evidence compels a confession of ignorance.[50]

It may well be, as Jugie has suggested, that the total object of the Byzantine feast comprised (*a*) the falling asleep of our Lady, that is, her departure from this world by a natural death; (*b*) her resurrection and glorious Assumption in body and soul, or, at times, the translation of her incorruptible body to the terrestrial paradise; and (*c*) the unceasing mediation of Mary in heaven for us.[51] At any rate, the fact of her death was basic to the Oriental feast. This is evident, first, from the pastoral letter, *The Dormition of Our Lady,* in which John, Archbishop of Thessalonica, introduced the Feast of the Dormition into his diocese *ca.* 620, shortly after Maurice prescribed it for the Empire: "Almost all the earth celebrates in festive fashion the annual remembrance of her repose—save for a few places, including . . . Thessalonica."[52] It is clear, secondly, from the earliest extant Greek homilies for the feast of August 15, which were delivered by distinguished churchmen in the seventh and eighth centuries and reveal in one way or another what Andrew of Crete announced so simply in an exordium: "Today's feast is a mystery: its subject is the dormition of God's Mother and it transcends the power of speech."[53] It is inescapable, finally, if we turn to the properly liturgical texts stemming from the eighth and ninth centuries which have found their way into the Menaia of the Eastern Churches; such, e.g., as the canon of Cosmas the Hymnodist: "In conceiving God, O pure Lady, you carried off the prize of victory over nature. Still, in imitation of your Creator and Son, superior to nature you bow low to the laws of nature; that is why, though you die with your Son, you rise to live eternally."[54]

[20]

In the West it was Rome which first received the Byzantine feast, perhaps as late as Pope Sergius I (687–701), with the August 15 date and the original title, Dormition of the Mother of God.[55] From Rome the feast soon penetrated into England and Gaul. As in the East, so in the West, the object of the feast was to commemorate the death of Mary and her entrance into glory. Originally it was the *dormitio* that had precedence: Mary's departure from this world by a natural death. But in time the *assumptio* gained the ascendancy: first, and quickly, the sheer title without a corresponding shift of emphasis in content; then, more slowly, a stress on the underlying idea of *assumptio,* though its precise nature is not always perlucid and the death-theme is never forgotten.[56]

The considerable role played by Mary's death in the late-patristic Western feast is evident from the liturgical books. The Roman, or Gregorian, Sacramentary which Adrian I sent to Charlemagne in 785–786 has the well-known *Veneranda* and *Subveniat* prayers for Assumption Day:

Venerable in our eyes, O Lord, is this feast day, on which the holy Mother of God submitted to temporal death, yet could not be weighed down by death's fetters—she who gave birth of her own self to your Son, our Lord, in flesh.

Let come to the aid of your people, O Lord, the prayer of God's Mother; though we know that she has departed this life (*migrasse*) conformably to the condition of the flesh, may we experience her intercession for us in the glory of heaven.[57]

If the Gelasian Sacramentary of the seventh century speaks only of our Lady's Assumption, vaguely and with no reference to its antecedent phenomena,[58] the Frankish

Gelasian Sacramentary of the eighth century has the *Veneranda* prayer, with its unmistakable admission of Mary's death.[59]

Still more precious because less laconic is the seventh-century Gallican liturgy as represented by the so-called "Gothic Missal." The Introit for the Assumption, underscoring Mary's uniqueness, declares that even her "death has found no parallel to match it."[60] The *Collectio post nomina* argues that "by reason of the Assumption she did not experience the defilement that follows on death," and urges the brethren to "beg the Lord that the dead may be released from the lower regions to the place where the body of the Blessed Virgin was transferred from the tomb."[61] The Preface, honoring "the day on which the Virgin Mother of God departed this world for Christ," proclaims that "she did not incur contamination from corruption, she did not undergo dissolution in the grave."[62]

Briefly, at the close of the patristic age we are confronted with a liturgical feast, (*a*) whose object, at least in part, is the departure of Mary from this world by a natural death; (*b*) which is strikingly widespread in East and West; and (*c*) which in some areas is almost two centuries old. Without suggesting that the infallibility of the Church is engaged here, without implying that we are faced with something genuinely irreformable, I submit that the liturgy of the dormition conveys a conviction of the teaching Church, the ordinary magisterium, in the middle of the eighth century—and that conviction is: our Lady died a natural death.

This conviction creates two urgent problems for the theologian. First, does the Feast of the Dormition in patristic times constitute the death of Mary an application of the theological adage, *lex supplicandi statuit legem credendi*? Apparently not. The one legitimate interpretation of the adage is the sense it carried at its birth fifteen centuries ago: that which is the direct object of the Church's petition in her official prayers cannot fail to be in conformity with revealed truth, with Catholic doctrine.[63] Concretely, the adage does not canonize the liturgy in its completeness. Its concern is a prayer, not a nocturn; and, within the prayer, its focus is precisely the petition. Splendidly pertinent is the *Subveniat* prayer. What the adage as such guarantees is the intercessory power of God's Mother in glory: "may we experience her intercession for us in the glory of heaven." The adage as such does not touch the peripheral affirmation: "though we know that she has departed this life conformably to the condition of the flesh."[64]

There is a second, more importunate problem to which the Feast of the Dormition awakens the theologian. Is the question of Mary's death a sheerly historical issue, and so the exclusive province of the historian, or is it theological as well, and so legitimately open to the proper activity of the theologian and the magisterial manifesto of the Church? The majority of Catholic scholars confess that the problem is authentically theological. In fact, whatever their solution to the problem—whether they conclude that Mary died or that she was immortal (by right or in reality or both)—their conclusion is reached almost invariably from theological premises and not from historical evidence.[65] However that may be, the liturgy of the dormition in the patristic age leaves a clear-cut impression that in the mind of the contemporary Church the death of Mary was a fact not simply historical but genuinely theological, because the liturgy links it to truths that are undeniably theological. Thus, the Adrian-Gregorian Sacramentary derives our

Lady's death from the existential mortality of human flesh.[66] A Menaion of the Eastern Churches represents Mary's death as analogous to, imitative of, the death of her Son.[67] And often enough the liturgy's concept of Mary's incorruption— a theological concept because supernatural—involves an immunity specifically from the corruption of the *grave*. In other words, the theological concept of Mary's incorruption included the lifelessness of her body and was meaningless without it.[68]

★ 4 ★

Greek Homiletic Literature

A fourth source of patristic testimony on the destiny of
Mary is the Greek homiletic literature of the seventh and
eighth centuries—a literature inspired by the feast of August
15 and influenced in varying degrees by the apocryphal accounts.[69] Among the earliest extant homilies of this sort is
the *Panegyric for the Dormition of God's Mother,* which
has come down to us under the name of St. Modestus,
Patriarch of Jerusalem († 634).[70] Remarkable for its
Christological and soteriological content, its conscious inde-
pendence of the apocrypha (which it does use), its reason-
able conjectures, and its repeated, unhesitating affirmation
of the Assumption, the homily leaves no doubt that Mary
died: "She fell asleep, she fell asleep, she fell asleep, she who
gave birth to the world's life and resurrection."[71] "Ever
anguished by the divine desire with which as Mother of
God she yearned for Him, the blessed Mary quit her holy
body with her eyes upon Him, and into His hands she com-
mended her all-blessed, all-holy soul."[72] Why did she die?
"As His mother all-holy, she followed Him. . . ."[73] In a
word, Mary died, in imitation of her Son.

Equally categorical in affirming our Lady's death and
anticipated resurrection is Germanus, Patriarch of Constantinople († 733), one of the most illustrious representa-
tives of Byzantine Mariology, unmatched as doctor of
Mary's universal mediation. Addressing his flock in the first
quarter of the eighth century,[74] he recognizes that she died,

[25]

though her death resembled a sleep, though her spirit was separated from her flesh "in wakefulness," though her migration was a "living sleep." [73] The reasons for her death are several. In the first place, Mary submits to "the death that is inevitable for human nature"; [76] she is asked by her Son to "give to the earth without distress what is the earth's"; [77] "it was fitting for the grave to welcome its own compound, human as it is." [78] In the second place, Germanus assigns a reason of a higher order. This death of Mary, the natural effect of her human condition, was preordained by God as an unanswerable corroboration of the Incarnation, of the reality of her Son's humanity:

> You have departed from earth for a proof—as a guarantee that the awesome mystery of the Incarnation was not an imaginary thing, in order that your own departure from transitory life might create belief that the God who was born of you came forth perfect man, Son of a genuine mother, inasmuch as she was subject to the laws of natural necessity, to the bidding of God's decree, to the exigencies of our span of life. You have a body like the rest of us, and so you could not but encounter the common death of men, just as your own Son and God of all did Himself . . . taste a like death in the flesh. . . . [79]

In a word, Mary died, because of the community of her nature with ours, and as a confirmation of the reality of the Incarnation.

A contemporary of Germanus named Andrew (✝ 740), native of Damascus, monk in Jerusalem, deacon in Constantinople, Metropolitan of Gortyna on the island of Crete, has left a trilogy of sermons for August 15, which he delivered on one day, perhaps in 717 or 718, probably in his episcopal see, in a church dedicated to the Virgin. [80] Andrew states flatly that the direct object of the feast is "the dormition of God's Mother"[81]—though it becomes obvious that the essential elements of the celebration involve as well the incorruption and translation of her body.[82] He records a tradition (*logos*) that Mary's death took place in extreme old age.[83] He notes that she died on Mount Sion, where she had always lived,[84] and was buried in Gethsemane.[85] He finds her death an "incredible" fact;[86] the death of Life's mother is an antinomy analogous to her virginal motherhood.[87] To rationalize the paradox, Andrew has recourse to Christ. Just as in His case the Genesis curse on humankind could not be completely abrogated, and He who was like us in all save sin "had to manifest all the marks of humanity,"[88] so Mary too had to "obey nature's laws and fulfil the dispensation which Providence fixed irrevocably on us from the first."[89] Andrew, therefore, does not discover in Mary a liability to death contracted by original sin; but neither does he suggest an authentic right to immortality somehow renounced.[90] As he sees it, Mary died because she too was subject to the physical laws which govern the human composite; for "it was proper to her nature to pay the debt common to all."[91] "If . . . there is no human being who 'shall live and not see death' (Ps 88:49), and if she whose praises we sing today is a human being and more than human, surely it is patently proven that she too has fulfilled the selfsame law of nature as we, though not in equal measure but in a fashion superior to us and not for the same reason which compels us to experience it."[92] Her death, like her life and her childbearing, was superhuman;[93] her migration, like her parturition, was "miracle-laden"[94]— from the death that resembled the ecstatic sleep of Adam,[95] through the incorruption of her body, to its final translation.

Another trilogy of sermons for the Feast of the Dormition was preached by John Damascene about the year 740, probably at Gethsemane.[96] Like Germanus, but with greater discretion, he makes use of apocrypha, especially John of Thessalonica. With the candor of Andrew he confesses that the circumstances surrounding his account of Mary's end are conjecture or rhetoric. But the sheer fact of her death is undeniable. It is cause for astonishment, yes: "Is it true that the source of life, that the Mother of my Lord, died?"[97] Moreover, her death, like her childbearing, was a painless thing;[98] it is more aptly titled "falling asleep" or "journey abroad" or a change of "residence."[99] But John does not dream of denying it. Basically, she died not in punishment for sin contracted, but because as a daughter of Adam she inherited from her first parents a mortal body which was taken from earth and had to return to earth. There are suasive reasons as well: (*a*) to keep Mary from being regarded a goddess, and (*b*) because even her Son, who took from her a mortal body, did not decline death. The pertinent texts are expressive:

The source of life is transferred to life by way of death! She who outstripped the limits of nature in her childbearing, bows now to nature's laws: her undefiled body is subjected to death! For incorruption is to be put on when mortality itself has been put off (cf. 1 Cor 15:53), seeing that even the Lord of nature did not refuse to experience death.[100]

She who poured forth to all men the life that is real, how could she be subject to death? The fact is, she yields to the legislation of her own Son, and as daughter of the ancient Adam she submits to the chastisement inflicted on her father; for even her Son, Life itself, did not refuse it.[101]

It was then, it was then that Adam and Eve, the parents of

[28]

our race, sent up that thrilling cry from gladsome lips: "Blessed are you, daughter; for you have removed from us the penalty for the transgression. You inherited from us a corruptible body, yet you gave birth for us to incorruption's garment. . . ." How is it that you will taste death, O immaculate one? For you, death will be a bridge to life, a ladder to heaven, a ferry to immortality.[102]

Depart, Lady, depart. Do not, after the manner of Moses, ascend and [then] die; rather die and in that way ascend. Commit your soul to the hands of your Son; restore to the earth what is the earth's. . . . See, the Virgin, Adam's daughter and God's Mother, transmits her body to the earth because of Adam; her soul she sends up to heaven's home because of her Son. . . .[103]

It is after this fashion that we recognize in this Virgin the Mother of God, and so celebrate her dormition. We do not call her a goddess (we will have none of that; this sort of story is Greek claptrap); for we proclaim her death as well. But we do recognize her as Mother of God-made-flesh.[104]

To sum up. The dormition orators of the seventh and eighth centuries affirm with one voice and with no hesitation that our Lady died. More than that, they are apparently unaware of a tradition to the contrary. Still more importantly, they are the first to venture explicitly a theology of Mary's death; and their approach is engaging.[105] Instead of distinguishing two aspects within death itself—the penal and the natural—they distinguish two aspects in Mary. As Mother of God, as Mother of Life, as Immaculate, and so on, we would expect her to be exempted from nature's universal law of death; but as descendant of Adam she should pay (though not for the same reason) her tribute to the sentence of death leveled at all humanity. The antinomy is resolved by recourse to reasons of a higher order—reasons which advised against a dispensation from the law. Two reasons in particular attract the Byzantine preachers. (1) Mary is a member of the fallen human family; as such, she inherits a mortal body. Providence has thought it wise to have her share the fate of that family in her body—a fate not unseemly, as we know from the example of her Son. (2) The death of Mary was to be a crushing refutation of docetism and a splendid confirmation of the Incarnation.

The reasons may not be compelling; few reasons are, where God's free choice is engaged. But the theologically significant fact is this: the Fathers in question affirm our Lady's death not primarily on the basis of speculative reasoning; they affirm it because the Church in her liturgy has affirmed it—has affirmed it with the Feast of the Dormition.[106]

Western Witnesses from Ephesus
to Bede

From Ephesus to Bede, Western witnesses on our problem are surprisingly scarce: two Jerusalem itineraries, Gregory of Tours, Isidore of Seville, the abbot Adamnan, and Bede himself.[107] The anonymous itinerary known as *Breviarius de Hierosolyma,* most probably to be dated about 500, mentions a basilica and tomb of Mary "near that pinnacle of the temple where Satan tempted our Lord Jesus Christ."[108] The *Itinerarium* falsely ascribed to Antoninus Placentinus but actually written by one of his companions (*ca.* 570) tells of a basilica of Mary in the Valley of Gethsemane "which they say was her home, in which she was taken up out of the body."[109] Gregory, writing from Tours in 590 and borrowing in all probability from a Syriac *Transitus* of the fifth century, describes Mary's death, burial, and Assumption in sober fashion:

After this, the Apostles scattered through different countries to preach the word of God. Subsequently, blessed Mary finished the course of this life and was summoned from the world; and all the Apostles were gathered together, each from his own area, at her home. On hearing that she was to be taken up from the world, they kept watch with her. All at once her Lord came with angels, took her soul, delivered it to Michael the Archangel, and disappeared. At daybreak, however, the Apostles lifted up the body together with the funeral-bed, placed it in a tomb, and kept watch over it, in readiness for the Lord's coming. And again, all at once the Lord stood by them and ordered the holy body taken up and carried on a cloud to paradise. There, reunited with the soul, it rejoices with His elect and enjoys eternity's blessings which will never end.[110]

In the seventh century, Isidore, Archbishop of Seville in Spain († 636), simply attests our profound ignorance on the manner in which Mary left this earth:

Some affirm that she quit this life by suffering a cruel, violent death. Their reason is that Simeon . . . said: "And your own soul a sword shall pierce." As a matter of fact, we do not know whether he was speaking of a material sword or of God's word that is powerful and keener than any two-edged sword. The point is, however, that no narrative informs us that Mary was slain by the punishment of the sword, seeing that nowhere is there an account even of her death. Some do say, though, that her tomb is to be found in the Valley of Josaphat.[111]

Isidore echoes Ambrose: we have no evidence that Mary died a martyr. He echoes Epiphanius too: we have no information at all about her death. We learn from Isidore that the thesis of Mary's martyrdom still persists; we learn, too, of a Jerusalem tradition on her tomb—a tradition which he is content to record without comment.

On the basis of a pilgrimage undertaken by the French Bishop, Arculf, between 670 and 685, Iona's Abbot Adamnan († 704) speaks of an "empty tomb" of Mary in the Valley of Josaphat, wherein she "rested after her burial. But how or when or by what persons her dear holy body was taken from this tomb, or where it awaits resurrection, no one (so we are told) knows for certain."[112] In his own book on the Holy Places, Venerable Bede († 735) mentions the reputed death of Mary on Mount Sion,[113] and borrows from Adamnan when he speaks of the "empty tomb, in which holy Mary is said to have rested for a while; but who took her away, or when, we do not know."[114]

★ 6 ★

Tradition of the Virgin's Tomb

The evidence presented in the preceding section, scant and unsatisfactory though it is, has the merit of introducing us naturally to a final facet of our problem: the claims of Jerusalem and of Ephesus to the tomb of Mary.

It is the contention of Jugie that the existence of a tomb of the Virgin in Jerusalem or its environs was utterly unknown before 570.[115] To begin with, he rejects as legendary the narrative in the *Euthymiaca historia* that the sovereigns of Byzantium, Marcian and Pulcheria, desirous of having the body of Mary for a church of the Virgin in Constantinople, addressed themselves to the Patriarch Juvenal of Jerusalem and to the other Palestinian bishops gathered in the royal city for the Council of Chalcedon (451): "We hear that in Jerusalem is the first and remarkable church of the all-holy Mother of God, Mary ever virgin, in the place called Gethsemane, where the body that brought life was buried in a coffin. We want to have her remains brought here for the protection of this imperial city." In reply, Juvenal relates what he has learned about Mary's passing "from an ancient and utterly unerring tradition." This includes her death, her burial in Gethsemane, and the discovery after three days of a coffin empty save for burial shrouds. Thereupon Marcian and Pulcheria ask Juvenal for the coffin and garments, and place them in the Church of the Mother of God in the Blachernae quarter of Constantinople.[116]

[35]

To support his thesis, Jugie adduces (*a*) the positive affirmations of Epiphanius and Timothy of Jerusalem; (*b*) the significant silence of pilgrims like Etheria and Eucherius, Jerome and Paula and Eustochium, even Leo the Great; and (*c*) testimonies, from the second half of the fifth century to the middle of the sixth and beyond, which speak of a house of Mary in Gethsemane, of a church in her honor there, but say nothing of a tomb. Jugie claims that the original tradition of Jerusalem simply put the *house* of our Lady in Gethsemane; that and naught besides. In the last years of the sixth century, or at the beginning of the seventh, Mary's house was located a half-hour from Gethsemane, on Sion, even in the Cenacle where Christ had celebrated the Last Supper and the Holy Spirit had descended upon the Apostles; from then on, Gethsemane and the Valley of Josaphat enclosed the *tomb* which had received her virginal body. The reason for the topographical change Jugie finds in the apocrypha: their need of a sufficient distance between death-place and burial-ground to permit the episode of the hostile intervention of the Jews and the incident of the Jew Jephonias. Sion was chosen because of the solemn mysteries that had been enacted therein; the Valley of Josaphat, because it was "the valley of judgment," where God was to judge all peoples till the end of time; more precisely Gethsemane, because it had been immortalized by the Saviour's agony.[117]

Other scholars disagree radically. They suggest that, in view of the temperate narrative and the similarity to Epiphanius' approach, the Juvenal story may well be substantially historical;[118] that there is strong support for the affirmation therein that the church erected at Gethsemane between the Council of Ephesus and the Council of Chal-

[36]

cedon contained as a sacred memorial the sepulchre of Mary.[119] They insist that Epiphanius, though uncertain of Mary's death, is completely intelligible only if he knew of *a* Jerusalem tradition that Mary died and was buried.[120] They recall that the paragraph from Timothy of Jerusalem may well not come from Jerusalem at all or even from the fourth century;[121] that it does not necessarily deny Mary's death;[122] that, in any case, Timothy's testimony does not of itself constitute a tradition.[123] They remind us that the argument from silence is significant only if the writers in question ought to have spoken. In the instance of Etheria, not only are we confronted with a considerable lacuna in the MS precisely where the good Spanish pilgrim might have spoken of a Jerusalem *grave*.[124] Where she speaks of the Jerusalem liturgy, she mentions only the sacred sites connected with that liturgy; and so she does not mention a *sanctuary* of the dormition, because at that time (393–396) a sanctuary did not exist.[125] Eucherius, writing about the middle of the fifth century, does not pretend to offer a complete description of the Holy Places; and the same should be said of Jerome, of Paula and Eustochium, of Leo's letter to Juvenal.[126]

These scholars are confessedly swayed by the testimony of the *Breviarius de Hierosolyma* and Ps.-Placentinus.[127] They are affected by the unanimity with which the apocryphal accounts locate the death of Mary in Jerusalem.[128] And they are much impressed by the verdict of the archaeologist H. Vincent that history and archaeology are in harmony in dating the construction of the Church of the Sepulchre of the Virgin between 450 and 460.[129]

Was there a tradition before 431 which localized in Gethsemane the grave of God's Mother? It would seem a defensible inference from the existence of the shrine; but we are not justified in asserting it apodictically. I am drawn to Gordillo's modest affirmation that "before the middle of the fifth century, when the public cult of the Virgin Mother of God began, the faithful of Jerusalem visited the grave of holy Mary in Gethsemane; and this grave confirmed them in their belief that our Lady died. . . . This silent testimony was the more convincing because in the bosom of the Church of Jerusalem no voice had been raised to deny the death of God's Mother."[130]

As warmly if not as widely debated is Ephesus' claim to Mary's tomb. Here the cruces of evidence and interpretation are two: the date of the Evangelist John's departure for Asia, and a letter from the Fathers of Ephesus (431) to the clergy and faithful of Constantinople.[131] On the first of these issues, only conjecture is possible. Some scholars, for example, are persuaded that John did not leave Palestine for Asia until a rather late date, even as late as the Jewish War (66–70); by that time Mary was surely dead, and so she never saw Ephesus.[132] Others see no good reason for prolonging John's sojourn in Palestine to advanced age; they find a late and relatively brief apostolate in Asia irreconcilable with his Asian fame; they prefer Tillemont's dual hypothesis: a lengthy residence in Ephesus beginning about 66, and an earlier visit when John would have brought Mary there; and there she died.[133]

The evidence of the Ephesus letter is more tangible. The pertinent sentence remarks that Nestorius had arrived earlier than others in Ephesus, *entha ho theologos Iōannēs kai hē theotokos parthenos hē hagia Maria*.[134] The problem, paradoxically enough, does not lie with the absence of a verb. The omission, if deliberate (and there is no cause to suspect otherwise), is acceptable Greek; we simply supply some form of the verb "to be." The problem is the meaning of "John" and "Mary." One interpretation insists that the clause has no reference to a sojourn or dormition or relics of John and Mary in Ephesus; it designates simply the principal church of Ephesus by the names of its titular patrons.[135] Others retort that the Council never speaks of churches in precisely that way; they observe that the church of the Council was simply the Church of St. Mary—the Church of St. John was distinct, though attached; they argue that the natural sense of the clause calls for the presence of John and Mary in Ephesus. It is certain, they say, that the Apostle lived and died there; the same is therefore affirmed of the Virgin.[136]

The evidence for Ephesus is meagre, vague, equivocal. It does not justify a confident affirmation, though it may permit a temperate conjecture, that before 431 a tradition existed which localized the grave of our Lady in Ephesus.[137]

⋆ Conclusion ⋆

From the evidence of the patristic age there emerges a widespread conviction of the early Church that our Lady died a natural death. This conviction, especially between the fifth and eighth centuries, was shared by hierarchy and faithful, preached by theologians, publicly affirmed in the liturgy. There is no comparable conviction to offset it; for in dissent we find only individuals, not a tradition. However, the nature of much of the evidence—sporadic comments before Ephesus, apocrypha obscure in origin and impalpable in weight, a feast still hidden in history—is too fragile to sustain an apodictic conclusion on the theological significance of this conviction. But the conviction is there. More than that, the consistency of its liturgical expression and the uniformity of its homiletic articulation warrant the conclusion that it was conscious, abiding, and informed.

★ Notes ★

[1] Among the more useful and comprehensive presentations of the patristic evidence, cf. M. Jugie, *La mort et l'Assomption de la sainte Vierge: Etude historico-doctrinale* (Vatican City, 1944); O. Faller, *De priorum saeculorum silentio circa Assumptionem b. Mariae virginis* (Rome, 1946); C. Balić, *Testimonia de Assumptione beatae Mariae virginis ex omnibus saeculis. Pars prior: Ex aetate ante Concilium Tridentinum* (Rome, 1948); A. Rivera, "La muerte de María en la tradición hasta la Edad Media (siglos I al VIII)," *Estudios marianos* 9 (1950) 71–100; L. Sibum, "La mort et l'Assomption de Marie," *Revue apologétique* 62 (1936) 424–45, 529–49, 652–63 (the last section is primarily speculative). See also J. A. de Aldama, "La muerte de la Santísima Virgen, según una obra reciente," *Estudios eclesiásticos* 21 (1947) 291–321 (a critique of Jugie's volume); and F. Cavallera, "A propos d'une enquête patristique sur l'Assomption," *Bulletin de littérature ecclésiastique* 27 (1926) 97–116 (a strong criticism of the methods and conclusions of Jugie's earlier "La mort et l'Assomption de la sainte Vierge dans la tradition des cinq premiers siècles," *Echos d'orient* 29 [1926] 129–43).

[2] Origen, *Comm. in Ioannem*, frag. 31 (*GCS* 10, 506). The fragment which contains this sentence is taken from catenae on John. Regrettably, the passage is found among the fragments (1–105) whose authenticity is questionable; cf. R. Devreesse, "Chaînes exégétiques grecques," *Supplément au Dictionnaire de la Bible* 1 (Paris, 1928) 1198–99. C. Vagaggini, *Maria nelle opere di Origene* (Rome, 1942) p. 128, regards as certain the "general authenticity" of the whole fragment, on the basis of parallel texts on Mary's perpetual virginity; but this does not guarantee the genuinity of individual phrases like "until her death."— In the abstract, *mechri teleutēs* could mean simply "until the end"; but it would be farfetched to suggest that in this concrete instance "end" and "death" were not identified in the mind of the author.

[3] Cf. Jugie, *op. cit.*, p. 57. Rivera, *art. cit.*, p. 85, observes justly that testi-

mony to Mary's death is not deprived of all value simply because an author takes her death for granted, affirms it in passing 'or incidentally; he notes a tendency in Jugie to depreciate such testimony unduly.

4 Ephraem, *Hymni de beata Maria* 15, 2 (ed. Lamy 2, 583). E. Beck labels spurious these Syriac hymns *De Maria* (Lamy 2, 519–641), in harmony with his general principle which denies to Ephraem all works which stress Mary's virginity in childbearing; cf. "Die Mariologie der echten Schriften Ephräms," *Oriens christianus* 40 (1956) 22.

5 De Aldama, *art. cit.*, p. 300, does not admit that the affirmation is incidental; the terms are antithetical: Mary remained virgin despite her maternity, and her body continued incorrupt despite her death.

6 Gregory of Nyssa, *De virginitate* 14 [13] (ed. J. P. Cavarnos, in W. Jaeger, *Gregorii Nysseni opera* 8/1, 306; PG 46, 377). The clause, *kat' autēn egeneto*, is difficult to translate because of the ambiguity inherent in *kata*. It may mean (*a*) death was "near" her, came close to her, as I have turned it above, in harmony with Jugie, *op. cit.*, pp. 62–63; or (*b*) death came "against" her, attacked her, as Balić would have it, *op. cit.*, p. 8—a translation which does not affect my interpretation of the passage; or even (*c*) death came "in quest of" her; but this seems excluded by Gregory's viewpoint: he envisions death as coming in quest not of Mary but of Christ.

7 In fact, L. Sibum, *art. cit.*, p. 544, finds Mary's death "explicitly affirmed" by Gregory. As he sums up Gregory's thought (cf. p. 439), the Virgin died, but her death is no hindrance to the dazzling victory she won when death was crushed on the fruit of her virginity.

8 Epiphanius, *Panarion*, haer. 78, 10–11 (*GCS* 37, 461–62).

9 *Ibid.* 78, 23 (*GCS* 37, 474).

10 Some, like Faller, *op. cit.*, p. 42, believe that Epiphanius personally favored the third hypothesis, a translation to glory without the prelude of death. Others, like Cavallera, *art. cit.*, pp. 110–12, find Epiphanius helpless before all three hypotheses; or, like Balić, *op. cit.*, p. 12, find it impossible to decide whether Epiphanius' doubt is genuine or fictitious.

11 So E. R. Smothers is inclined to believe; cf. his sober study, "Saint Epiphanius and the Assumption," *American Ecclesiastical Review* 125 (1951) 355–73, esp. 371.

12 Cf. Jugie, *op. cit.*, pp. 73–74.

13 *In prophetam Simeonem* (ed. Faller, *op. cit.*, p. 26; cf. PG 86, 245).

14 Cf. Jugie, *op. cit.*, pp. 74–76. His exegesis that Mary did not die is apparently based on what might be considered the "obvious" meaning of "immortal": exempt from death. That this exemption was not a provisory, temporary thing stems from his preferred interpretation of *analēpsimois chōriois*: she has been transported "to the place where Jesus is since His ascension."

15 Cf. B. Capelle, *art. cit. infra* note 17, pp. 25–26. That Mary did not die Capelle concludes from the context; that she may still die he concludes from the restrictive "to this day."

16 Cf. Faller, *op. cit.*, pp. 30–31: "immortal," of itself, says nothing about

the past; we too shall be immortal after the resurrection of our bodies, despite the death that will have preceded (cf. Balić, p. 10: immortality does not necessarily exclude death; e.g., in the case of Christ). Nor does "to this day" call into doubt the perpetuity of the immortality, because immortality is of its very concept perpetual, and she who is "to this day" immortal through the assumption effected by her Son will certainly not die later; "to this day" is simply an Oriental manner of speaking, analogous to the *donec* in Mt 1:25. To which Capelle responded that the restrictive *donec* has meaning only when there is question of things subject to alteration; you do not say that a triangle has angles "to this day." "To this day" has no meaning if "immortal" means definitive immortality in glory; we do not say that St. Benedict is among the elect "to this day." "Tout l'Orient n'y peut rien changer" (*art. cit.,* p. 25).

[17] Cf. B. Capelle, "Les homélies liturgiques du prétendu Timothée de Jérusalem," *Ephemerides liturgicae* 63 (1949) 5–26. Jugie was not impressed by Capelle's argumentation; cf. *L'Immaculée Conception dans l'Ecriture sainte et dans la tradition orientale* (Rome, 1952) p. 74 and note 3 *ibid.;* he continued to consider Timothy a contemporary of Epiphanius.

[18] Severian of Gabala, *In mundi creationem* 6, 10 (*PG* 56, 498).

[19] Hippolytus, *In psalmum* 22; quoted by Theodoret, *Eranistes,* dial. 1 (*PG* 83, 88; cf. also *PG* 10, 610, 865).

[20] So too Balić, *op. cit.,* p. 5.

[21] Ambrose, *Expositio evangelii secundum Lucam* 2, 61 (*CSEL* 32/4, 74).

[22] Ambrose, *De institutione virginis* 7, 49 (*PL* 16, 333).

[23] Jerome, *Adversus Rufinum* 2, 5 (*PL* 23, 447).

[24] Jerome, *Contra Ioannem Hierosolymitanum* 31 (*PL* 23, 399).

[25] Jerome, *Epist.* 75, n. 2 (*PL* 22, 687).

[26] Perhaps more significant than his ambiguous speech is Jerome's silence. Though he knew the local traditions of the Holy Land as well as did Epiphanius, he gives no indication that he is aware of any historical tradition with reference to the death or grave of our Lady; cf. B. Altaner, "Zur Frage der Definibilität der Assumptio B.M.V.," *Theologische Revue* 44 (1948) 133–34. But the argument from silence is a delicate weapon.

[27] Cf. Paulinus, *Epist. 50,* nn. 17–18 (*CSEL* 29, 419–23). The same letter is contained among the letters of Augustine, *Epist. 121,* nn. 17–18 (*CSEL* 34/2, 737–42).

[28] Cf. Augustine, *Epist. 149,* n. 33 (*CSEL* 44, 378–79).

[29] Augustine, *In Ioannis evangelium* 8, 9 (*Corpus christianorum,* ser. lat. 36, 88; *PL* 35, 1456): "Commendat matrem discipulo; commendat matrem prior matre moriturus, et ante matris mortem resurrecturus. . . ." *De catechizandis rudibus* 22, 40 (*PL* 40, 339): "virgo concipiens, virgo pariens, virgo moriens. . . ." *Enarratio in psalmum 34,* serm. 2, n. 3 (*PL* 36, 335): "Etenim ut celerius dicam, Maria ex Adam mortua propter peccatum, Adam mortuus propter peccatum, et caro Domini ex Maria mortua est propter delenda peccata." It has been asserted by T. Gallus that, if these three texts are carefully analyzed, they will yield a different conclusion; cf. "Ad testimonium 'explicitum' s. Augustini

de morte b. Virginis," *Divus Thomas* (Piacenza) 30 (1953) 265–69. The crucial text for his thesis is the *Enarratio* passage. Three codices do not mention Mary's death, two of them reading: "Maria ex Adam, Adam mortuus propter peccatum. . . ." This reading, Gallus insists, is preferable from the context (it does not involve a tautology incompatible with "celerius," as does the traditional reading) and from Augustine's doctrine elsewhere (he refused to speak of sin in connection with Mary; and, for him, death in us is the result of sin in us, and so the traditional reading would mean that Augustine burdened Mary with original sin). This, he argues, makes it more probable that in the other two passages "virgo moriens" and "prior matre moriturus et ante matris mortem resurrecturus" do not express the concrete fact of Mary's death but are excellent rhetorical devices for, respectively, her perpetual virginity and the proximity of Christ's death and resurrection. The argument is closely reasoned but, apart from the fact of variants in the codices, seems to put a strain on scholarly credulity.

[80] Balić, *op. cit.*, p. 13, finds the hypothesis of a peaceful death "generally speaking, in tranquil possession." The exceptions (certainly Epiphanius and perhaps Timothy) are important, but it is difficult to assess their significance. G. M. Roschini, "Il problema della morte di Maria SS. dopo la Costituzione Dogmatica 'Munificentissimus Deus,'" *Marianum* 13 (1951) 152, asserts that the Timothy text remains, "nel suo senso ovvio, una testimonianza di prim'ordine, unita a quella di S. Epifanio, in favore della immortalità di Maria. Questa è la primitiva tradizione sulla fine dell'esilio terreno di Maria. Valgono più queste due testimonianze negative che centinaia di testimonianze affermative di una cosa ritenuta ovvia, comune." I would suggest (*a*) that the attitudes of Epiphanius and Timothy are not the clear denials of Mary's death so transparent to Roschini; (*b*) that it is gratuitous to claim that "*this* is the primitive tradition on the end of Mary's earthly exile"; and (*c*) that the principle—the denials of two writers, even men of the stamp of Epiphanius and Timothy, is worth more than hundreds of witnesses who take something for granted—is difficult of demonstration. On the one hand, the very fact that early theologians do not dream of excepting our Lady from the common lot is itself significant; on the other, we may apply to Epiphanius and Timothy what Sibum has asserted of the latter alone: "As a single swallow does not make a spring, so the lone witness of Timothy does not make a tradition" (*art. cit.*, p. 543).

[81] Cf. the valuable accounts in Jugie, *op. cit.*, pp. 101–71; Balić, *op. cit.*, pp. 14–65 (East), 137–53 (West); A. C. Rush, "The Assumption in the Apocrypha," *American Ecclesiastical Review* 116 (1947) 5–31; *id.*, "Assumption Theology in the Transitus Mariae," *ibid.* 123 (1950) 93–110.

[82] Cf. Jugie, *op. cit.*, pp. 103–5; Balić, *op. cit.*, pp. 14–15. Some, in the wake of Tischendorf, find the origins of the *Transitus* in a Greek prototype which may go back to the fourth century, therefore considerably before Ephesus; cf. E. Amann, "Apocryphes du Nouveau Testament," *Supplément au Dictionnaire de la Bible* 1 (Paris, 1928) 483. Others look to a Syriac original of the second half of the fifth century; cf. Jugie, pp. 107–8.

[33] Ps.-John the Evangelist, *Liber de dormitione sanctae deiparae* 39 (ed. C. Tischendorf, *Apocalypses apocryphae Moisis, Esdrae, Pauli, Iohannis. Item Mariae dormitio, additis evangeliorum et actuum apocryphorum supplementis* [Leipzig, 1866] p. 108). Tischendorf placed this apocryphon in the fourth century, or even earlier; cf. *ibid.*, prol., p. xxxiv. Jugie, however, dated it between 550 and 580; cf. *op. cit.*, p. 117.

[34] *Liber de dormitione sanctae deiparae* 44–45 (ed. Tischendorf, pp. 109–10). On the difficult exegetical problem of the lot of Mary's body after death, cf. Balić, *op. cit.*, pp. 18–23.—Even more explicit is the Greek account of John, Archbishop of Thessalonica (*ca.* 620). John's Prologue declares that "some time after each of the Apostles had set out, at the command of the Holy Spirit, to preach the Gospel in the whole world, the all-glorious virgin Mother of God left the earth by a natural death" (*Dormitio dominae nostrae deiparae ac semper virginis Mariae* 1 [*PO* 19, 375–76]). And the apocryphon itself declares that "she fulfilled her dispensation, with her face turned to the Lord in a smile" (*ibid.* 12 [*PO* 19, 396]).

[35] Cf. L. Leroy, "La dormition de la Vierge," *Revue de l'orient chrétien* 5 (1910) 162. My translation is based on the Latin version of Balić, *op. cit.*, p. 49. The date of the Arabic translation of Greek Ps.-John is uncertain. The Arabic writer is not always faithful to his Greek model, but interpolates extraneous elements, especially from Syriac accounts.

[36] *The Obsequies of the Holy Virgin* (ed. and tr. W. Wright, *Contributions to the Apocryphal Literature of the New Testament* [London, 1865] pp. 46–47); the Latin translation by Balić, *op. cit.*, pp. 30–31, differs only on minor points. One of the MSS of this epilogue seemingly dates from the second half of the fifth century; cf. Jugie, *op. cit.*, pp. 107–8. Jugie thinks it an original product of Syriac circles, probably Jacobite.

[37] *Liber transmigrationis Mariae* (*CSCO* 39, 29, 43–44; Latin translation *ibid.* 40, 24, 38–39). For the Syriac model cf. Jugie, *op. cit.*, pp. 120–22.

[38] Theodosius of Alexandria, *De dormitione Mariae* 5 (ed. F. Robinson, in *Texts and Studies* 4/2 [Cambridge, 1896] 106; translation *ibid.*, p. 107).

[39] Theodosius, *ibid.* (ed. Robinson, pp. 106–8; translation based on Robinson's, pp. 107–9). In the Bohairic account of Ps.-Evodius, *On the Falling Asleep of Mary*, a query of Peter and the other disciples, as to whether it is not possible for Mary never to die, is answered by Christ: "I wonder at you, O my holy Apostles, for this word which you have just spoken. Can the word which I uttered in the beginning prove a lie? No, God forbid! In the beginning I pronounced a sentence upon all flesh, that all must needs taste death. Because of the flesh that I took, I also tasted death . . ." (n. 8; translation based on Robinson's, *op. cit.*, p. 55).—For other Coptic accounts cf. Jugie, *op. cit.*, pp. 126 ff., and Balić, *op. cit.*, pp. 38 ff.; also Robinson, pp. 25 ff.

[40] *Dormitio sanctae deiparae* 1 (German translation by P. Vetter, "Die armenische Dormitio Mariae," *Theologische Quartalschrift* 84 [1902] 328–29). The text was published in Venice in 1898 by I. Dayetsi. This *Transitus* seems to depend in part on John of Thessalonica.

[41] Ps.-Melito, *Transitus sanctae Mariae* 7–8 (ed. Tischendorf, *op. cit.*, pp. 129–30; translation based on Balić, *op. cit.*, pp. 139–40). There is wide divergence of scholarly opinion on Ps.-Melito's sources (whether Syriac or Greek) and time of composition (fourth or fifth century: most authors, e.g., Cabrol, Turmel, Cocaud, Capelle, Merkelbach, Faller, Gordillo; end of fifth century or beginning of sixth: Le Hir, Chatain; about 550: Jugie, *op. cit.*, p. 112).— Codex V (Silos 2, saec. 11) of the redaction called *Transitus Mariae C* suggests that Mary's death is a consequence of Adam's sin; ed. A. Wilmart, in *Studi e testi* 59 (1933) 342, in the critical apparatus.

[42] Thus, John of Thessalonica speaks of a primitive account of Mary's death composed by eye-witnesses of the event and its accompanying prodigies; cf. *Dormitio Mariae* 1 (*PO* 19, 376). But there is no good reason to credit the existence of such a document.

[43] J. A. de Aldama has shown, against Jugie, that the hypothesis of natural death was the least likely to appeal to the authors in question. He concludes that the only sufficient explanation of such unanimity is that the writers "found themselves faced with an earlier tradition so clear, so universal, so closely knit to the faith of their Churches in the glorification of God's Mother that they saw themselves compelled to put it at the basis of their legendary descriptions." He believes it brings us back to the beginning of the fourth century or the end of the third; cf. *art. cit.*, pp. 294–98. Cf. also Rivera, *art. cit.*, pp. 79–84: the apocrypha invite our consent to the fact of Mary's death; they are based on an oral tradition which goes back to the Apostles.

[44] Some worthwhile studies on the origins and development of the Feast of the Dormition are: Jugie, *op. cit.*, pp. 172–212; W. O'Shea, "The History of the Feast of the Assumption," *Thomist* 14 (1951) 118–32; B. Capelle, "La fête de l'Assomption dans l'histoire liturgique," *Ephemerides theologicae Lovanienses* 3 (1926) 33–45; *id.*, "L'Assunzione e la liturgia," *Marianum* 15 (1953) 241–76; V. Gonzáles, "La dormición de María en las antiguas liturgias," *Estudios marianos* 9 (1950) 63–69.

[45] It is Jugie's opinion, *op. cit.*, p. 174, that the Dormition was an outgrowth, in many Churches, of the Commemoration (*memoria*), in which it was contained virtually. The original solemnity celebrated Mary's *dies natalis*, her entry into the Church Triumphant; but, in the absence of any certain data from Scripture or tradition on the way whereby this entry was effected, the Church celebrated her virginal motherhood and her role as New Eve, recalling the Gospel accounts of the Annunciation, Visitation, and Nativity. The first rift in this reticence was effected when the *Transitus* stories popularized the death of Mary with its attendant marvels; then it was that the Commemoration tended to be transformed into the Dormition and Assumption of Mary. Further impetus was given to this transformation by the development of a cycle of Marian feasts (Annunciation, Nativity of Mary, Anne's Conceiving), which had to be rounded out by a feast emphasizing her end and destiny. Cf. also B. Capelle, "La fête de la Vierge à Jérusalem au Vme siècle," *Muséon* 56 (1943) 1–33.

[46] Cf. the Syriac Ps.-James, *Six Books on the Dormition*, with its triple commemoration of the Virgin, on alleged instructions of the Apostles: December 27, May 15, and August 13. The Syriac text and an English translation were published by W. Wright, in *Journal of Sacred Literature* 6 (Jan., 1865) 419–48; 7 (April, 1865) 129–60.

[47] Cf. Theodosius, *De dormitione Mariae* (ed. Robinson, *op. cit.*, pp. 90–127). According to Jugie, *op. cit.*, pp. 132–33, some of the sixth-century Severian Monophysites, to corroborate their thesis of the corruptibility of Christ's body, subjected His mother to the corruption of the tomb for a time (206 days in *De dormitione Mariae*); this would explain the two feasts, death and Assumption. But Balić, *op. cit.*, p. 46, note 1, argues convincingly that Theodosius does not submit Mary's body to actual corruption; her body is simply called "naturally mortal," "naturally corruptible."

[48] Cf. the synaxary of the Ethiopian Church for August 22 (an amplification of Theodosius' account), edited by I. Guidi, *Le synaxaire éthiopien, III: Mois de Nahasê et de Pâguemên*, in *PO* 9 (1913) 335–40 (French translation by S. Grébaut).

[49] This decree is mentioned by the medieval historian, Nicephorus Callistus, *Ecclesiastica historia* 17, 28 (*PG* 147, 292).

[50] The decree seems to have encountered opposition in certain quarters, partially because of the feast's kinship with the apocrypha, possibly also because of its Monophysite ancestry. John of Thessalonica reports *ca.* 620 that his predecessors refused to adopt it because of the falsifications in the *Transitus* tales; cf. *Dormitio dominae nostrae* 1 (*PO* 19, 376). The Church of Jerusalem, in the seventh and eighth centuries, accepted the feast but kept the older designation, the Commemoration; cf. Jugie, *op. cit.*, pp. 181–82, with his references to the seventh-century canonarium of Jerusalem; also F. M. Abel, in *Revue biblique* 11 (1914) 455.

[51] Cf. Jugie, *op. cit.*, p. 185.

[52] John of Thessalonica, *Dormitio dominae nostrae* 1 (*PO* 19, 376). From the context it is obvious that "repose" is equivalent to what John calls her "natural death" (*ibid.*).

[53] Andrew of Crete, *In dormitionem sanctissimae deiparae dominae nostrae oratio* 2 (*PG* 97, 1072). The sentence which follows immediately, "It is a mystery that in the past (*ēdē*) was celebrated by few, but now (*nūn*) is honored and loved by all," is difficult to reconcile with the declaration of John of Thessalonica that "almost all the earth celebrates" it. Jugie, *op. cit.*, p. 235, note 2, suggests an alternative interpretation: the feast has been and still is celebrated publicly by a small number, but the dormition which is its object is known and honored by all. L. Carli prefers to see a situation peculiar to Crete, where the feast would have declined from an earlier splendor; cf. *La morte e l'Assunzione di Maria santissima nelle omelie greche dei secoli VII, VIII* (Rome, 1941) p. 63.

[54] Cosmas, *Ode 1, Strophe 4*, in the office of *Orthros* (*Menaei totius anni*,

[49]

m. aug. 15, Vol. 6 [Rome, 1901] 413). A good selection of passages from the Menaia pertinent to Mary's death and Assumption is given by Jugie, *op. cit.,* pp. 188–93, and by Balić, *op. cit.,* pp. 67–72.

⁵⁵ The earliest reference to such a feast at Rome is to be found in the notice on Sergius in the *Liber pontificalis,* ed. L. Duchesne, 1 (Paris, 1886) 376: "Constituit ut diebus Adnuntiationis Domini, Dormitionis et Nativitatis sanctae Dei genetricis semperque virginis Mariae ac sancti Symeonis, quod Ypapanti Greci appellant, letania exeat a sancto Hadriano at ad sanctam Mariam populus occurrat." Jugie believes that Sergius may well have introduced the four feasts into the Roman calendar; cf. *op. cit.,* p. 196, note 1.

⁵⁶ Cf. Jugie, *op. cit.,* pp. 202–11.

⁵⁷ H. Lietzmann, *Das Sacramentarium Gregorianum nach dem Aachener Urexemplar* (Münster i. W., 1921) p. 88; H. A. Wilson, *The Gregorian Sacramentary under Charles the Great* (London, 1915) p. 97. Cf. the same texts in *PL* 78, 133; Migne reproduces (cols. 25–240) the edition of U. Ménard (Paris, 1641). On the authorship, date, content, character, development, MSS, and editions of the Sacramentaries, cf. A. Bugnini, "Sacramentario," *Enciclopedia cattolica* 10, 1558–69; J. A. Jungmann, *The Mass of the Roman Rite: Its Origins and Development,* tr. F. A. Brunner, 1 (New York, 1951) 44–47, 60–63. The Gregorian Sacramentary was a papal feast-day and stational missal, not primarily a book for ordinary parish services. Its origins may be traced with high probability to Gregory the Great (590–604), but in the seventh and eighth centuries the original underwent many changes.

⁵⁸ Cf. H. A. Wilson, *The Gelasian Sacramentary. Liber sacramentorum Romanae ecclesiae* (Oxford, 1894) pp. 193–94. The same prayers, with minor variants, are to be found in *PL* 74, 1174; Migne reproduces (cols. 1055–1244) the edition of L. A. Muratori, *Liturgia Romana vetus* (Venice, 1748; reprinted 1760, 1772).

⁵⁹ Cf. K. Mohlberg, *Das fränkische Sacramentarium Gelasianum* (Münster i. W., 1939) p. 168; also Wilson, *The Gelasian Sacramentary,* p. 353. The "eighth-century Gelasian" is a syncretistic sacramentary fashioned within the Frankish Church about 750, probably at the urging of King Pepin. Its base is the earlier Gelasian (the papal sacramentary which originated at the end of the fifth century and entered Gaul shortly before the middle of the sixth), but it has added elements from the Gregorian and local sacramentaries; cf. Bugnini, *art. cit.,* col. 1565.

⁶⁰ Cf. H. M. Bannister, *Missale Gothicum. A Gallican Sacramentary* 1 (London, 1917) 30; also J. Mabillon, *De liturgia Gallicana libri III* (Paris, 1729) p. 211 (reproduced in *PL* 72, 244). In his article, "Sur la provenance du 'Missale Gothicum,' " *Revue d'histoire ecclésiastique* 37 (1941) 24–30, G. Morin argued persuasively that the Missal stems from the monastery of Gregorienmünster in Alsace towards the year 700. Its primary importance is that the *Missale Gothicum* and the *Missale Gallicanum vetus* which completes it are "the two best sources of information on the formulas in use in the

Frankish Church in the seventh century for the celebration of the Eucharistic Sacrifice" (*ibid.*, p. 24).

[61] Cf. Bannister, *op. cit.*, pp. 30–31; Mabillon, *op. cit.*, p. 212; *PL* 72, 245.

[62] Cf. Bannister, *op. cit.*, pp. 31–32; Mabillon, *op. cit.*, pp. 212–13; *PL* 72, 245.

[63] The adage is contained in a document long circulated unjustifiably under the name of Pope Celestine I (423–432), *De gratia Dei indiculus seu praeteritorum sedis apostolicae episcoporum auctoritates,* a collection (perhaps made by Prosper of Aquitaine) of official documents of the Holy See on the Pelagian controversy, followed by some pertinent liturgical considerations; cf. *PL* 50, 531–37, esp. 535: " . . . obsecrationum quoque sacerdotalium sacramenta respiciamus, quae ab apostolis tradita, in toto mundo atque in omni ecclesia catholica uniformiter celebrantur, ut legem credendi lex statuat supplicandi. . . ." The examples of Christian petition which follow in the text reveal the sense of the last clause.—A pertinent excursus of Pius XII in the Encyclical, *Mediator Dei (AAS* 39 [1947] 540–41), refutes the Modernist interpretation of the axiom, which would make liturgical experience, liturgical fruitfulness, the touchstone of doctrinal truth. In the Pope's analysis, the role of the liturgy is to bear public witness to the faith of the Church. Hence, Catholic faith is mirrored in, not determined by, the liturgy.

[64] Such, substantially, is likewise the mind of Jugie, *op. cit.*, pp. 523–25.

[65] I say "*almost* invariably" because there are scholars who, e.g., believe we can get back to apostolic times and apostolic tradition through the apocrypha; cf. note 43 above.—For the problem, and some approaches to its solution, cf. B. Aperribay, "La muerte de la Santísima Virgen, problema meramente histórico o también teológico?", *Estudios marianos* 9 (1950) 17–42; Bernardo de la Inmaculada, "La muerte de María, exigencia de su gracia santificante," *ibid.*, pp. 125–73; E. Sauras, "La muerte de María y la gracia de corredención," *ibid.*, pp. 175–212; M. Cuervo, "El dogma de la Inmaculada y la muerte de María," *ibid.*, pp. 213–25; J. A. de Aldama, "La muerte de María y el concepto integral del misterio asuncionista," *ibid.*, pp. 227–38; B. Farrell, "The Immortality of the Blessed Virgin Mary," *Theological Studies* 16 (1955) 591–606.

[66] Cf. references in note 57 above.

[67] Cf. Cosmas the Hymnodist, cited in note 54 above.

[68] Cf. the citations from the Gallican liturgy, notes 60–62 above; also the selections from the Menaia and from the Latin liturgy in Balić, *op. cit.*, pp. 67 ff., 155 ff.

[69] Several earlier post-Ephesus texts are unjustifiably cited in favor of Mary's deathlessness. Thus, the assertion of the Jerusalem priest Hesychius (✝ after 450) that the Virgin is "a tree of incorruption and a garden of immortality" (*De sancta Maria deipara sermo* [*PG* 93, 1465]) is actually a reference to the virginal maternity that brought forth the "blossom undecaying" which is Christ. The phrase of another priest of Jerusalem, Chrysippus (✝ 479), "the ever-green

shoot of Jesse" (*Oratio in sanctam Mariam deiparam* 1 [*PO* 19, 336]), is too vague to support the suggestion of Jugie, *op. cit.*, p. 76, that it is a probable allusion to Mary's immortality. A redaction of the Ps.-Prochorus recension (between 450 and 500) of the *Acta Ioannis* (Cod. Vatic. graec. 654, fol. 95a; cf. Jugie, p. 88) states that "the holy Mother of God passed from life to life, from this transient life to eternal life"; *pace* Jugie, the sentence says nothing on the way in which Mary passed from life to life. On the other side of the picture, the line from Ps.-Dionysius (between 490 and 531), "we came together to contemplate the body that gave Life its beginning and received God" (*De divinis nominibus* 3, 2 [*PG* 3, 681]), though understood of Mary's body with more or less certainty since Maximus the Confessor and Andrew of Crete, bristles with too many difficulties to be confidently employed as testimony to her death; cf. the reservations of Jugie, *op. cit.*, pp. 99–101.—We should mention here the metrical homily of the Syrian poet, James of Sarug (451–521), on the burial of Mary; cf. the edition of P. Bedjan, *S. martyrii, qui et Sahdona, quae supersunt omnia, syriace. Accedunt homiliae Mar Iacobi in Iesum et Mariam syriace* (Leipzig, 1902) pp. 709–19; and the Latin translation, on a later MS, by A. Baumstark, in *Oriens christianus* 5 (1905) 82–89. Apparently too early to have been originally a homily for the Feast of the Dormition, it nevertheless does speak of Mary's death and the obsequies; she is buried on the summit of Mt. Olivet.

[70] Doubt has been cast on the authenticity of the *Panegyric*. Thus, for reasons stylistic and historical, theological and topographical, Jugie believes that the author lived far from Jerusalem and wrote after the Monothelite controversy, at the end of the seventh or the beginning of the eighth century; cf. *op. cit.*, pp. 215–19. Carli, however, sees no reason to question its authenticity; cf. *op. cit.*, p. 31; see pp. 32–42 for an analysis of the homily and an appraisal of its sources and value.—I say, "among the earliest homilies" is that of Modestus, because A. Wenger has rather recently published a contemporary or earlier panegyric preached by Theoteknos, bishop of Livias (about thirty-five kilometers east of Jerusalem), for the Marian feast of August 15, which he designates *analēpsis;* cf. *L'Assomption de la T. S. Vierge dans la tradition byzantine du VIᵉ au Xᵉ siècle: Etudes et documents* (Paris, 1955) pp. 96–110, 271–91. Composed between 550 and 650 (more probably the second half of the sixth century), this discourse may be the first genuinely Catholic affirmation of the glorious Assumption. Theoteknos is equally clear on the fact of Mary's death: "for, if the God-bearing body of the holy one tasted death, nevertheless it did not suffer corruption" (*Encomium* 15 [Wenger, p. 278]).

[71] Modestus, *Encomium in dormitionem sanctissimae dominae nostrae semperque virginis Mariae* 12 (*PG* 86, 3308). He conjectures that Mary died on Mt. Sion and was buried in Gethsemane; cf. *ibid.* 4, 9, 13 (*PG* 86, 3288, 3300–3301, 3312).

[72] *Ibid.* 11 (*PG* 86, 3308).

[73] *Ibid.* 12 (*PG* 86, 3308).

[74] Germanus, *In sanctae Dei genitricis dormitionem*. For sheerly practical reasons we retain the Migne division into three homilies: *PG* 98, 340–48, 348–57, 360–72; actually, the so-called "Homilies 1 and 2" are simply two parts of one sermon. For the date—certainly before 729, very probably before 726, possibly *ca.* 717–18—cf. Carli, *op. cit.*, pp. 45–46.

[75] Cf. Germanus, *In dormitionem sermo* 3 (*PG* 98, 368); *Sermo* 2 (*PG* 98. 348); *Sermo* 1 (*PG* 98, 340). Mary's death takes place in Jerusalem, in the house of St. John; her burial, in Gethsemane.

[76] *Sermo* 2 (*PG* 98, 357).

[77] *Sermo* 3 (*PG* 98, 361).

[78] *Sermo* 2 (*PG* 98, 357).

[79] *Sermo* 1 (*PG* 98, 345). Note the same argument in the Coptic apocryphon of Theodosius of Alexandria, *De dormitione Mariae* 5 (ed. and tr. Robinson, *op. cit.*, pp. 106–9).

[80] Andrew, *In dormitionem sanctissimae deiparae dominae nostrae*. Here, again for practical reasons, we retain the order of Migne, *PG* 97: *Oratio 1*, cols. 1045–72; *Oratio 2*, cols. 1072–89; *Oratio 3*, cols. 1089–1109. Internal evidence and the majority of MSS suggest strongly that the actual order of delivery was 2, 1, 3; cf. Carli, *op. cit.*, pp. 61–62; Jugie, *op. cit.*, p. 234, note 2. On the place and date, cf. Carli, pp. 60–61; also Andrew, *Oratio 1* (*PG* 97, 1045): "this venerable temple of God's Mother." For the probable thesis that in this period trilogies on our Lady, delivered the same day before the same audience, were not an exception, cf. C. Chevalier, "Les trilogies homilétiques dans l'élaboration des fêtes mariales, 650–850," *Gregorianum* 18 (1937) 361–78; on Andrew, pp. 368–72; Germanus, pp. 372–77; Damascene, pp. 362–67.

[81] *Oratio* 2 (*PG* 97, 1072); also *Oratio* 3 (*PG* 97, 1088).

[82] Cf., e.g., *Oratio* 2 (*PG* 97, 1080).

[83] Cf. *Oratio* 1 (*PG* 97, 1060).

[84] Cf. *Oratio* 2 (*PG* 97, 1073); also *Oratio* 1 (*PG* 97, 1064).

[85] Cf. *Oratio* 1 (*PG* 97, 1064).

[86] *Oratio* 3 (*PG* 97, 1089).

[87] Cf. *Oratio* 1 (*PG* 97, 1069).

[88] *Ibid.* (*PG* 97, 1048).

[89] *Ibid.* (*PG* 97, 1053).

[90] Cf. Carli, *op. cit.*, pp. 67–68.

[91] *Oratio* 3 (*PG* 97, 1092).

[92] *Oratio* 1 (*PG* 97, 1053).

[93] Cf. *Oratio* 2 (*PG* 97, 1080).

[94] *Ibid.* (*PG* 97, 1085).

[95] Cf. *Oratio* 1 (*PG* 97, 1052). For Andrew's attempt to explain the absence of an authentic tradition on the migration of Mary, cf. *ibid.* (*PG* 97, 1060); and for his argument from the "empty tomb," *Oratio* 2 (*PG* 97, 1081–84).

[96] For the text of the three homilies, *In dormitionem celebratissimae*

gloriosissimaeque ac benedictae dominae Dei genitricis semperque virginis Mariae, cf. *PG* 96, 700–721, 721–53, 753–61. Their authenticity is commonly admitted today, especially on the basis of the MS tradition; cf. Carli, *op. cit.,* pp. 77–78.

[97] *Homilia* 3, n. 3 (*PG* 96, 757).

[98] Cf. *Homilia* 2, n. 3 (*PG* 96, 728).

[99] *Homilia* 1, n. 10 (*PG* 96, 716).

[100] *Ibid.* (*PG* 96, 713).

[101] *Homilia* 2, n. 2 (*PG* 96, 725). In translating "submits to," I presume that the PG reading *hypererchetai* (col. 725) is a copyist's error for *hyperchetai.*

[102] *Ibid.,* n. 8 (*PG* 96, 733).

[103] *Homilia* 3, n. 4 (*PG* 96, 760).

[104] *Homilia* 2, n. 15 (*PG* 96, 744). On the question whether Damascene recognized in Mary a right to immortality, cf. the categorical affirmation of C. Chevalier, *La mariologie de saint Jean Damascène* (Rome, 1936) pp. 199–200, and the rebuttals by Carli, *op. cit.,* p. 83, and Balić, *op. cit.,* pp. 86–87.

[105] For the following summation I am much indebted to the shrewd insights of Carli, *op. cit.,* pp. 107–9.

[106] One might also consult with profit the four homilies on the dormition from the pen of Cosmas Vestitor, though he belongs to the second half of the eighth century; for the Latin text in which they are extant, cf. A. Wenger, *op. cit.,* pp. 313–33.

[107] We have already spoken of the Latin *Transitus* of Ps.-Melito, variously dated from the fourth century to the sixth; cf. note 41 above.—I do not see a reference to anything but natural sleep in the lines of the poet Venantius Fortunatus, writing before 576: "Quot vigiles turmae, cum te sopor altus haberet, Solaque dormitans tot vigilare dares?" (*Miscellanea* 8, 7 [*PL* 88, 281]).

[108] *Breviarius de Hierosolyma* (*CSEL* 39, 155). For the date cf. M. Gordillo, "La muerte de María madre de Dios en la tradición de la Iglesia de Jerusalén," *Estudios marianos* 9 (1950) 55 and note 85 *ibid.* Jugie, *op. cit.,* p. 684, would place the work in the last years of the sixth century, or even in the seventh.—On the *Breviarius* cf. also A. Wilmart, "Un nouveau témoin du Breviarius de Hierosolyma," *Revue biblique* 37 (1928) 101–6.

[109] Ps.-Antoninus Placentinus, *Itinerarium* 17 (*CSEL* 39, 170). Balić, *op. cit.,* p. 172, note 1, has uncovered the weakness in Jugie's argument, *op. cit.,* p. 92, that another reading, substituting "de qua eam dicunt ad caelos fuisse sublatam" (*CSEL* 39, 203) for "in qua et de corpore sublatam fuisse," is the primitive text.

[110] Gregory of Tours, *Lib. 1 miraculorum: In gloria martyrum* 4 (*PL* 71, 708).

[111] Isidore, *De ortu et obitu patrum* 67, 112 (*PL* 83, 148–49). A later redaction states even more clearly that the sword is a spiritual thing, and presents the existence of the Jerusalem tomb as absolutely certain; cf. *PL* 83, 1285–86.

[112] Adamnan, *De locis sanctis* 1, 12 (*CSEL* 39, 240).

[113] Cf. Bede, *Liber de locis sanctis* 2 (*CSEL* 39, 306).

[114] *Ibid.* 5 (*CSEL* 39, 309).

[115] Cf. Jugie, *op. cit.,* p. 681.

[116] *Euthymiaca historia* 3, 40; found in Damascene's *In dormitionem Mariae homilia* 2, n. 18 (*PG* 96, 748–52). The *Historia* of which this is an extract has not been recovered. Many scholars consider the extract an interpolation in Damascene's homily. Jugie insisted that it should not be dated much before 890; cf. *op. cit.,* pp. 159–67. Wenger, *op. cit.,* p. 137, asserts that Jugie has convincingly demonstrated the apocryphal character of the Juvenal story, but he observes justly that the MS Sinaït. gr. 491, the oldest witness of the *Historia,* forbids us to date the legend later than 750.

[117] Cf. Jugie, *op. cit.,* pp. 681–87.

[118] So M. Gordillo, following Kekelidze, Abel, and Baldi; cf. *Mariologia orientalis* (Rome, 1954) p. 222 and note 45 *ibid.*

[119] So D. Baldi, "La tradizione monumentale della dormizione a Gerusalemme," *Studia Mariana* 1 (1948) 131–36.

[120] So Faller, *op. cit.,* p. 53.

[121] So Capelle, in *Ephemerides liturgicae* 63 (1949) 5–26.

[122] So Faller, *op. cit.,* pp. 30–31; also Balić, *op. cit.,* p. 10.

[123] So Sibum, *art. cit.,* p. 543.

[124] Cf. the beginning of the text of Etheria (= Sylvia), *Peregrinatio ad loca sancta* (*CSEL* 39, 37); and *ibid.* 17 (*CSEL* 39, 60): " . . . cum iam tres anni pleni essent, a quo in Ierusolimam venissem . . . ."

[125] Cf. *ibid.* 24–49 (*CSEL* 39, 71–101).

[126] Cf. Eucherius, *De situ hierusolimitanae urbis atque ipsius Iudaeae epistola ad Faustum presbyterum* (*CSEL* 39, 125–34); Jerome, *Epist.* 108 (*CSEL* 55, 306–51); Paula and Eustochium, *Ad Marcellam de sanctis locis* (*CSEL* 54, 329–44); Leo, *Epist.* 139, n. 2 (*PL* 54, 1105).

[127] Cf. notes 108 and 109 above; also Baldi, *art. cit.,* pp. 138–41.

[128] So M. Gordillo, in *Estudios marianos* 9 (1950) 46–52.

[129] Cf. Vincent's chapter, "Tombeau de la Vierge. Le monument," in H. Vincent and F.-M. Abel, *Jérusalem. Recherches de topographie, d'archéologie et d'histoire* 2 (Paris, 1922) 821–31, esp. 829. In Vincent's view, "a very modest oratory existing for scarcely twenty years in the Valley of Gethsemane safeguards the basic veracity which a sound critique cannot deny the *Historia euthymiaca.*" This would explain best how Juvenal could have interested the Emperor in an expensive expansion of the shrine.—For the literary evidence, one should not omit the chapter of Abel, "Le tombeau de la sainte Vierge," in the same volume, pp. 805–20, where the pertinent texts are reproduced. Cf. also Abel's "The Places of the Assumption," *Thomist* 14 (1951) 109–17.

[130] Gordillo, in *Estudios marianos* 9 (1950) 58.

[131] For Tillemont's argument based on the name "St. Mary" given to the cathedral church of Ephesus, cf. L. Heidet and L. Pirot, "Assomption," *Supplément au Dictionnaire de la Bible* 1, 645–47.

[132] So Jugie, *op. cit.*, p. 10. See Abel, "Le tombeau," p. 806, for the possibility that John may have left Jerusalem in 42 (on the morrow of James's martyrdom) or after 58 (when Paul was still evangelizing Ephesus); in either case Mary would have been advanced in years and, some argue, it is unlikely that John would have subjected her to so long and perilous a journey.

[133] So J. Euzet, "Le Père Jugie et la question du lieu où est morte la sainte Vierge," *Divus Thomas* (Piacenza) 26 (1949) 345–59, esp. 345–49.

[134] J. D. Mansi, *Sacrorum conciliorum nova et amplissima collectio* 4 (Florence, 1760) 1241.

[135] So Jugie, *op. cit.*, pp. 96–98; also Heidet-Pirot, *art. cit.*, col. 645.

[136] So Euzet, *art. cit.*, pp. 349–52.

[137] Cf. Abel, "Le tombeau," p. 808. For the significance of the "revelations" of Anne Catherine Emmerich with reference to the Ephesus tradition, cf. Heidet-Pirot, *art. cit.*, cols. 648–49.

⋆ Index ⋆

Date Due

	PRINTED IN U. S. A.		

Printed in the USA
CPSIA information can be obtained
at www.ICGtesting.com
LVHW080855060923
757276LV00003B/137